BIRDING

for

BABIES

A Numbers Book

by Chloe Goodhart
illustrated by Gareth Lucas

BACKYARD BIRDS

In your own backyard
there are plenty of birds to see.
Grab your binoculars and spy
one black-capped chickadee!

There are **two**
red-bellied woodpeckers,
busy drumming *tap-tap-tap*,
making a hole for a home
with their sharp beaks and red caps.

FACT

A red-bellied woodpecker can stick
out its tongue nearly two inches past
its beak!

Do you see those black birds,
you smart little birder?
Three American crows.
That's almost a murder!

Here's **four** blue jays
with their bright blue jackets.
Follow the noise to find them—
they make such a racket!

Blue jays often mimic the calls of
hawks to warn fellow blue jays or
to trick other birds.

See those familiar faces,
cheerful crests and orange bills?
Those are **five** northern cardinals
foraging their fill.

Who is clinging to the tree trunks
with white cheeks and
a belly that matches?
Count them as they creep on down,
six white-breasted nuthatches!

White-breasted nuthatches often start
at the top of a tree and inch down
headfirst looking for food such as
caterpillars and spiders.

There's a small flock of birds eating seeds from the feeder. **Seven** tufted titmice whistling *peter-peter-peter!*

Do you see **eight** northern mockingbirds looking for some grub? They flash their white wing patches as they dart from shrub to shrub!

FACT

Northern mockingbirds sing day and night, often mimicking other birds and even imitating sounds such as car alarms.

See **nine** American robins with their bright red chests.

Some are eating worms while some are building nests.

Robins don't eat the same kind of food all day long. They eat worms and bugs in the morning, and berries and fruit in the afternoon.

Ten American goldfinches are perched among the thistles.

Per-tee-tee-tee . . .

Listen to them whistle!

FACT

American goldfinches shed their feathers in late summer and again in late winter. When males return to their bright yellow color, it is a sign that spring is here.

First published in the United States of America
by Penguin Workshop, an imprint of
Penguin Random House LLC, New York, 2022

PENGUIN is a registered trademark and PENGUIN
WORKSHOP is a trademark of Penguin Books Ltd,
and the W colophon is a registered trademark of
Penguin Random House LLC.

Manufactured in China
Library of Congress Cataloging-in-Publication
Data is available.

ISBN 9780593386989
Special Markets ISBN 9780593661406 Not for resale

10 9 8 7 6 5 4 3 2 1

RRD

This Imagination Library edition is published by Penguin Young Readers, a division
of Penguin Random House, exclusively for Dolly Parton's Imagination Library,
a not-for-profit program designed to inspire a love of reading and learning, sponsored
in part by The Dollywood Foundation. Penguin's trade editions of this work are
available wherever books are sold.